CHASIA'S ENCHANTMENT
Expanded

CHASIA'S ENCHANTMENT

Expanded

Poems of WORLD PEACE, LOVE, & UNIVERSALITY

Hilda Chasia Smith

DURVILE & UpRoute
Calgary, Canada
DURVILE.COM

DURVILE & UpRoute

UPROUTE IMPRINT OF DURVILE PUBLICATIONS LTD.

Calgary, Alberta, Canada
durvile.com

LIBRARY AND ARCHIVES CATALOGUING IN PUBLICATIONS DATA

Chasia's Enchantment Expanded:
Poems of World Peace, Love & Universality

Smith, Hilda Chasia, author

1. Mindfulness & Meditation
2. Jewish Culture | 3. World Peace

Every River Lit Series, Ways of Light
Series editor, Lorene Shyba MFA PhD

ISBN: 978-199-0735-60-8 (print pbk)

Cover painting and paintings throughout the book:
Hilda Chasia Smith
Cover and book design: Lorene Shyba

Canada Alberta Government

Durvile Publications would like to acknowledge the financial support of
the Government of Canada through the Canadian Heritage Canada Book Fund
and the Government of Alberta, Alberta Media Fund.
Printed in Canada. First edition, first printing. 2022.

We acknowledge the traditional land of the Treaty 7 Peoples of Southern Alberta:
the Siksika, Piikani, and Kainai of the Niisitapi (Blackfoot) Confederacy; the Dene Tsuut'ina;
and the Chiniki, Bearspaw, and Wesley Stoney Nakoda First Nations.
We also acknowledge the Homeland of the
Otipemisiwak Métis Government of the Métis Nation within Alberta.

For

Lenny, Penny, Mandy,
Caleb, Zane and to our
extended family near and far.
This book is also for all people of the world
who uphold and work toward personal
and universal peace and love.

Contents
Chasia's Enchantment Expanded

Contents
Chasia's Enchantment Expanded

Contents
Chasia's Enchantment Expanded

Preface

I AM THRILLED AND HONOURED to have been asked to expand *Chasia's Enchantment*. This assignment is particularly meaningful to me, as I deeply appreciate the recognition and awards the first edition received in 2021 and 2022. As a recipient of several accolades, including Top Life Educator and Top Fearless Leader from the International Association of Top Professionals (IAOTP), I am eager to share my heartfelt motivations. My goal is to inspire you to recognize our urgent need to find solutions to eliminate unwarranted bias and hatred stemming from the conflict in the Middle East.

In this second edition of *Chasia's Enchantment*, you will find new poems and meditations marked with a heart in the top corner, as you see above. Additionally, artworks from the original edition, previously in black and white, are now published in colour, enhancing their beauty and impact. I believe this new presentation offers a more captivating way to experience the art.

Through me, a universal soul speaks, aiming to encourage world peace, universal love, equanimity, diverse unity, and healing ascensions—a fact reflected in the themes of the new material in the book. As inhabitants of this Earth, we are not different from one another. We share a plethora of emotions, feelings, and thoughts. We are one human family, though we often struggle to understand each other due to our cultural differences. Yet, we need each other to survive and thrive at levels of love unimaginable if we remain perpetually in a state of fear or flight. Aspire to love and be inspired by love in both thought and action. Your entire being will thank you, and you will be healthier, as will your family, friends, and everyone you meet.

As a woman born into a family of war-torn people, I am amazed at how deeply they lived, loved, and shared their talents, work ethic, and connectedness to all people, regardless of background, color, or religious beliefs. They taught me to learn as much as possible about the beautiful way of life I was born into, emphasizing the ethical truth: "Love thy neighbor as thyself. Do not do to another what you would not want to have done to yourself." As a first-born Canadian, I was deeply inspired by the diverse unity of people from all over the world who came to this country. Differences? Yes, but growing up in an observant family who followed their religion, I learned the freedom in limitation—limitation that allowed for limitless thinking, discussion, time for rest and relaxation, and inquiry.

Spending time with family and friends, engaging in interests, and attending a school with children from war-torn families provided every opportunity to learn and grow together with children from different backgrounds. The common thread was courtesy. What a blessing it was to be taught manners, courtesy, and respect for oneself and others as part of the religion and way of life I experienced. My parents were among the fortunate ones who survived the horrors of the Second World War and the Holocaust. Jewish people, having experienced profound suffering, are often empathetic to anyone or any group that suffers. They are not alone; all nations have suffered, and all people need peace, love, and friendship.

My parents had nightmares and screamed in their sleep with flashbacks of the war years. They did their best to shield this from their children, but we heard. The next day, they would say it was a bad dream, but it was in the past, and they would move forward, always striving to make a living, spend time with family, see friends when possible, and be good neighbours to people of many different backgrounds, cultures, religions, and ways of life. What a blessing to glean from both an old world and a new one.

Judaism, historically and biblically, is the first of three monotheistic religions. The Torah is a code of law not only for Jewish people but for the world on how to live a meaningful life. Kabbalah and Torah are interconnected, and studying them requires baby steps, much like a first-year university student wouldn't immediately understand doctoral-level work. We need great teachers in all areas of life and learning. A great teacher opens your mind to think critically—not to criticize but to examine what you are learning. Who is teaching you? What do they want you to believe, and why? Do you have the facts? Are they true?

Let your loving brain and heart lead you. Stay in touch with intuition through healthy stillness by actively listening. Most of the time, we are on autopilot. To stop the treadmill of knee-jerk reactions, we need to pause, breathe, centre ourselves, and stay open to the highest good for maximum potential in any moment. Be like water; flow.

It matters that the world has gone crazy and that Jewish people, along with others, are being attacked. The tragedy that befell, and is still befalling, innocent people in the Middle East is deeply saddening.

Protests expressing antisemitism are a terrifying resurgence of prejudice, echoing the horrors of the past. The Jewish people continually strive for dignity and wholeness. Let us open our hearts and replace hate with the universal values of love, peace, thoughtfulness, and kindness. Every child deserves to grow up free from being used as shields or compromised by their own people.

People of all nations: Palestinians, Arabs, Jews, Christians, First Nations, Africans—and the list goes on—deserve freedom from intergenerational trauma. Seek out healers, teachers, family members, friends, doctors, nurses, life coaches, therapists, and the wisdom of nature to find inner peace.

Perhaps, just perhaps, we will witness an end to war in our lifetime.

Shalom, Salam, Namaste, Paix, Paz. Peace.

— *Hilda Chasia Smith,*
Calgary, Alberta 2024

PART 1
Meditations

Durvile.com/Meditations.html

Unified consciousness
connects our smiles.
Everything else distracts from love's true path.
Love, the soul's currency, revealing our
true selves, abundant in creativity,
linked in the cosmic love field.
Awaken to your essence:
love, spirit, unity.
Every moment,
seek peace, love,
unity.

Unity Meditation

Sit down, feet planted on solid ground. Straighten your back. Shoulders, loose. Let your breath carry you into stillness. If the floor is your choice, lean back against the wall, legs crossed. Or lie down, find your comfort. We begin. Eyes shut softly. Focus on breath. Each inhale, each exhale, a step further into calm.

Hello, friends. Your smiles, a universal language. No judgment, no preconceptions. We all crave love, a gift beyond religion, beyond life, background, or colour. Respect our differences; we are currents, reacting, responding, training ourselves to solve conflicts, personal and universal, addressing pain with intention.

Fortify your heart with love, for self, for others. No one holds all answers for their lives, let alone the world. In each breath, possibility.

Stay curious. Listen with heart and soul to nature, to divinity. Seek loving-kindness, respect. Self-respect and love flow with grace, healing wounds, embracing creativity. Nourish minds, hearts, bodies, souls. Teach and learn love, understanding the sacred unity.

Unified consciousness connects our smiles. Everything else distracts from love's true path. Love, the soul's currency, revealing our true selves, abundant in creativity, linked in the cosmic love field. Awaken to your essence: love, spirit, unity. Every moment, seek peace, love, unity—*Shanti. Shalom. Salam. Paz.*

Feel the air move through you. Observe yourself: breath, body, thoughts, feelings. Step into love's spaciousness. Feel your body tingle, invited to live in loving consciousness. Daily, transform reactions into blissful responses to your world. Smile, universal soul, a magnet of love, life, karmic action. *Namaste.*

Unity meditation, your birthright. Float in it, heart-connected, spreading light in all directions, wishing for awakened love and unity. Start with you, I'll start with me, again and again, my friend. I love you. Turn strangers into friends, enemies into friends. Stay strong in unity meditation. Practice awakens love in body, spirit, heart, and soul. Come home to Unity consciousness. Walk it, talk it, listen, speak, think, feel, be it. One smiling breath at a time. I see you, hear you, feel you without touching, sense you.

Seated or lying down, eyes closed, mouth relaxed, body at ease. Light as a breeze, you are loved. This is unity consciousness. Rest in true being, body, mind, soul.

Deepen each breath, return slowly to normal breathing. Open your eyes, wiggle fingers and toes, hands on lap, softly smile, and say, Unity consciousness is mine, yours, ours, awakening. Awaken to the eternal within, the potential of Unity consciousness, in each breath.

Namaste, my friend. When ready, close this practice with three Oms, whispered, then louder. A deep breath, sound released, invigorating your life force with peace and joy.

Ocean's Breath, Love's Flow

Find a quiet place to sit or lie down. Elongate your back, relax your shoulders. Feel your sitting bones in contact with the chair, floor, sofa, or bed you are on. Breathe in and out through your nostrils, eyes closed. Sense the air entering and leaving your body in a slow, beautiful rhythm like a gentle, lovely dance.

Become aware of every part of your body relaxing. Your heart lifts into deeper ease with every breath. Allow the breath to fill your lungs, your entire rib cage in flow, expanding and contracting. Feel a little lighter, releasing any tension with each gentle, loving breath.

Now, let your breath change to the gentle sounds of waves on the ocean. Gently constrict the back of your throat, creating the sound of ocean waves with your breath. Let this natural rhythm bring you into a state of restful awareness and peace. Your parasympathetic system, your body's rest-and-digest system, finds ease and balance with each mindful breath. Allow your midsection to expand with each breath. Ebb and flow, ebb and flow.

You are the ocean of peace. You are an unconditioned spirit, a field of infinite possibility.

Breathe love. Breathe peace.
Breathe intelligent curiosity.

Breathe no judgment. Breathe relaxed alertness.
Breathe empathy.

Breathe loving kindness and compassion.
Breathe gentle strength.

Breathe respect. Breathe beauty.
Breathe healthy stillness. Breathe smiles.

Breathe tenderness. Breathe the wisdom of ancestors.

Breathe teachings of unified well-being.
Breathe godliness. Breathe equanimity.

Breathe understanding. Breathe care.
Breathe the sharing of skills and abilities.

Breathe support. Breathe cleanliness of body, mind, and spirit to refresh your heart and soul.

Rub your hands together, place them over your closed eyes for a minute. Now place your hands at your heart. Return to quiet breath. Breathe in peace, breathe out love. Set a living intention for the week. When you are ready, bring your arms to your sides.

Open your eyes as if for the first time. Wiggle your toes and fingers. Gently move your neck from side to side. Move your body a little.

Write down your loving intention for yourself and others. Keep a copy in your pocket or somewhere you can check daily. Continue with your day or evening, focusing on personal and universal love and peace. Glow with positive change for yourself and the world. Stand up for universal love and peace in each breath. Peace and love to you. Peace and love to the world. *Amen.*

Holding Hands Meditation

Hello, friends.

Sit down or lie down, find your comfort. Close your eyes, softly. Breathe slowly through your nose. As you breathe in peace, let a gentle smile form. As you breathe out, send that peace to yourself and the world.

Picture this: you are holding hands with a beloved relative. Look into their eyes. Just breathe together. Let whatever comes—smiles, tears, tenderness—be. Feel the love passing through your joined hands, heart to heart.

Now, hold hands with a child you love. Look into their eyes. Feel the warmth between you, the love radiating, filling both your hearts.

Imagine now holding hands with someone far away. Send your love across the distance. Let it fill their heart and yours.

Finally, hold hands with someone difficult to love. Send genuine care from your heart, no judgment. Feel your love wrap around them, pass through their heart.

This practice elevates your natural well-being. Your vital organs rest, not in flight or fight.

What others do matters, but not as much as your calm, loving response. Wonder, calm, helps us act with kindness and respect.

Breathe in harmony. Through your nostrils, breathe silently in. Breathe out with a gentle "haah." After twenty minutes, return to ocean breath or easy nostril breathing, mouth closed.

Stay curious, open to love. It's your essence, everyone's essence. The universe, the divine, nudges us to grow in love. May unified consciousness be our shared reality.

The Dolphin

Let's go on a little journey, a guided mediation to relax and refresh you, in every cell. Let's go for a walk by the ocean. It's a beautiful day—warm, the sand is warm. The waves are dancing, and you've come to this ocean. Sit down and relax. Take a nice slow breath in, and a slow breath out, as you relax your shoulders. Sit nice and straight as you listen to the beautiful waves as they play, allow yourself to relax even more with each beautiful inhale, and exhale. Imagine, that you have turned into a beautiful dolphin, and that you have entered this magnificent ocean filled with fish, and beautiful shells, and tiny little creatures of the ocean, dancing all around you. And you find there is a whole school of dolphins who have invited you to come and swim with them in the beauty of the deep blue ocean. And every dolphin is expressing their joy with their squeals and you are a part of it all. The sun is shining brilliantly on the ocean and the waves are dancing with you. And as you are sitting you. And as you are sitting on the shore imagining that you are that beautiful dolphin playing in the water, you can feel that you *are* one... breathing the air, in and out, gently. And a smile widens on your own lips at the shore as you breathe in and you breathe out, feeling every cell in your own body, as alive and as happy, and as joyful as the imagining of you, as a dolphin. Breathe in, deeply and slowly. Breathe out, deeply and slowly. With each breath, feel the energy of the ocean, in you. For you are the ocean of your own being. Simply breathe. And when you are ready, in your incredibly relaxed state of joy and being, put your hands to your heart, bowing to the ocean within you, the ocean in the world, all the oceans, and know that we are all a part of this magnificent universe, like the dolphins in the ocean.

Namaste. Shalom.

The White Feather

Repeat the beauty of breathing, slowly and deeply. Can you feel the difference between the air going in, and the air coming out? You might find a difference in the temperature, and smile in gratitude to this moment. Can you imagine stepping into a beautiful forest in the summertime? The trees are in full foliage and flowers of every colour are gently blowing in the wind, colours of the rainbow and beyond, fluttering their petals as if to say, "Welcome, so glad you are here." As you step into the forest, there is a beautiful pathway in front of you, a wide pathway of soft golden earth as if to say, "Come, come deeper into the forest." As you take a step you feel that the sun rays are falling even more enchantedly onto you, shedding their magnificent light all around you, as they have right through the forest. Allow yourself to walk in grace. And as you are walking, become even more aware of your breathing. Has it deepened a little bit? Allow it to. Let your lips turn into a radiant smile and know that you are part of the magic of life, of all this radiance. And as you are walking on the path, it turns to the right and you wonder. But allow yourself in that wonder to be carried by the path to wherever it is going. And as you look at the beautiful trees and the magnificence of the blue sky, you feel a soft warm breeze at your back. Suddenly, you hear the sound of water as you walk through the splendour of the forest. Butterflies and birds are dancing and singing. You can see them in the distance. A few butterflies have circled you in the joy of knowing you are there. As the water gets a little louder, you can see a river flowing and you walk to the edge of the beautiful bank of the river. As you look down to the river, you see a large white feather that is there in front of your feet. The lightness of the feather seems to magically rise and you reach your hand out and the feather lands right in your hand. This feather is a reminder of the lightness of your own being as you listen to the water sing a soft melody, you can feel the refreshment of your own heart and soul in every cell of your body radiating with this new energy and the reminder of the lightness of your own breath and your own being, for you are that. You return, feeling totally refreshed and at ease with the lightness of being that is beyond words as you walk back through the forest. Ageless child, you are a part of this magnificent world and universe and all that you are is within and around you. Let your spirit soar and as you hear those words, you open your arms with a feather in your hand, and slowly raise them as if you are an eagle and bring them down, standing firmly on the ground, moving in silence, bringing your hands to your heart with the feather. Knowing that you are safe, that you are whole, that you are loved, that you are strong. Remember, you are the river, you are the forest, you are the sky, you are the earth, you are everything. In the forest, may you be ever green all of your days, soaring like an eagle, with your feet planted firmly on the ground. *Namaste. Shalom.*

Shalom

This is a Jewish meditation. A meditation from the words of our *Siddur* that is read in the morning, in the evening, in the afternoon. This is a prayer thanking the divine and asking for peace for all Jews and all people in the world.

Oseh Shalom beemromahv
Hoo ya-aseh shalom alainu
vay uhl kol Israail v'eemru omain

May the one who brings peace to His universe
Bring peace to us and to all Israel.
And let us say, Amen.

Ya-ahseh shalom ya-ahseh shalom
shalom alainu v'kol ha-ansheem
v' eemru omain

Let there be peace. Let there be peace for all.
And let us say, Amen.

Guided Star Dream

Sit or lie down comfortably. Come with me on a journey through the stars on a beautiful clear night—a warm night in summer. Relax, breathe in, breathe out slowly, and with each breath, deepen your relaxation just a little more. As you float in the sky, allow yourself to be carried by the warm breeze and watch the stars twinkling as you breathe in the beautiful soft air, and know that you are radiating with those stars. As you breathe in and out, slowly deepen the stillness and the relaxation of your heart. And when you are ready, make your way back to your mat, your bed, or your chair — wherever you are. Wiggle your toes and your fingers. Become aware of exactly where your body is and breathe normally.

The Feminine Divine

Join me in a meditation of your feminine divine. Every person has a masculine divine and a feminine divine. In the ancient teachings of both Sanskrit and in Judaism, Sanskrit being a holy language of the Hindu people, and Lashon Kodish a Hebrew holy language of the Jewish people, we find Shakti, the feminine divine and Shekhinah, the feminine divine. The feminine divine is universal. Let us go on a journey of embracing the feminine divine within you, and me. Sit comfortably on a chair or on a mat, whatever it is you'd like to sit on — even a comfortable big rock, with your back nice and straight, with your head resting on your beautiful shoulders. Relax your shoulders. Lift your sternum towards the sky. Simply breathe, with your mouth closed, breathe in the fresh beautiful air around you that is constantly circulating in you, and back out into the world. With each breath, allow yourself to simply relax a little more. Imagine, that there is a beautiful light, a golden light in the centre of your heart and that light is permeating through your whole body. Watch it expand through every limb, from your feet, moving right through your legs, as you breathe slowly and deeply, feel that light warming you, gently. Feel that light, like a ball of light moving into your hips and into your lower abdomen, and all of your body, moving upward into your belly, into your heart again and into every organ and every part of your body. This light is illuminating you. There is the possibility of manifestation of whatever it is you that you need for health, wellness, prosperity, joy, connection, communication, peace, love, equanimity. And this light is moving into your throat, all the way again through your face, between your eyes, all the way through the crown of your head. And as you breathe in and out, feel the blessing of your breath, a gratitude for being able to breathe and being breathed by the divine. Of all that manifests and is manifested — feel the Shekhinah, and Shakti, the feminine divine of your own personal gender and awareness of who you are in the universality of your being. And imagine yourself now allowing a waterfall that suddenly appears in a beautiful mountain that you can imagine pouring all that beautiful energy, warmly, onto you. As you stand beneath the waterfall, whether you are dressed or whether you are in a bathing suit, or whether you have come there in your own skin, letting the water shine on you in the sunshine. Let all that needs to be washed away wash away on your body as you feel the sun. And the strength of the mountain, the presence of her healing surrounding you. The feminine divine within the mountain, within the earth, in water and within you, allowing yourself to feel refreshed and knowing that all is manifested is from the womb of life and choose that which brings you home to Mother Earth, that brings you to the Shakti, to the Shekhinah of who you are. See yourself coming right back to this moment on your chair or the big rock you might be sitting on, wherever you are, in the calmness of your beautiful breath, smile to your heart. Close your eyes, breathe gently for a minute or two, and open your eyes as if for the very first time. Peace, Shakti, Shekhinah.

Sleep, Derekh the Way

Join me in a guided meditation that may help you go to sleep more easily, more restfully. Sit down on a chair with your feet on the floor, or lie down on the ground or on your bed. Feel the earth beneath you and simply rest. Be able to breathe into your beautiful body a gift of air flowing in and flowing out, rhythmically, naturally. With your eyes closed, allow the music to bring just a little more quiet to you. With every breath to simply relax and sink more deeply into your own being. Let all the thoughts of the day float away like a cloud passing by, or a wave on the ocean that returns to the stillness of the ocean. Keep breathing slowly and deeply, allowing yourself to feel the beauty of your heartbeat. And when you are ready, let's find our way to the beauty of our hearts, you to yours, and me to mine, simply through the *derekh*, the way. Starting with your feet, allow yourself to feel, the best you can, the inside of your feet. Allow them to relax, completely. Moving to your ankles, feel the inside of your ankles relaxing, as we are all covered in this amazing encapsulating skin that supports everything inside. Feel your calves in the front of your legs relax completely. Moving to your knees, allow your knees to relax even more, doing nothing but imagining a deeper relaxation. Moving to your hips, feel them melt into the floor or the chair that you are sitting on. With each breath, allow yourself to simply be. If thoughts come to you, ideas, just let them float away for now and be with your magnificent breath. Relax your abdomen, feel yourself getting even more relaxed. Keep breathing deeply, and softly. Let your ribcage relax, in the front and in the back, knowing that every organ is relaxing and filling your body with rest, as you breathe into your body, and out. And as we make our way to our heart, feel a beautiful glowing light, expanding into every part of your body and you've made your way home to your heart, but you travel with that light now to your throat as your heart keeps expanding the light within you everywhere in the loving gracious fullness of your restfulness for that is the way of the *derekh*. And the light now fills your face and your ears and moves right to the top of your head as you melt even further into peacefulness, relaxation and the true beauty of who you are, in every breath. Take a nice deep breath and feel all of your body relaxing even deeper into the earth as you are supported above and below on the way on the *derekh* of life, always leading with your heart wrapped in the soul of life, wrapped in your own soul. *Laila Tov*. Good Night.

PART II
Inspirations

May no more war occur,
and may neighbours live in peace.
We must educate ourselves
and nations to speak
Of love, healing,
and the divine spark within us all.

Prayer for Peace

I wonder...
If we shared our time on Earth
as partners,
with each other,
all nations, nature's lessons,
imagination, intent, living beautifully,
trading evil for life, hate for peace, love?
What would happen if you stepped into the ocean
and mountains of pure possibility
to love and live with such blessing?

I wonder...
If we cast away negativity?
If we practiced common good, for ourselves
and each other, everywhere, always?
If we valued everyone's offerings?
If we saw others as ourselves,
no judgment, just curiosity?
If beautiful thoughts and feelings
shaped our beliefs and well-being?
If you knew your pure potential to simply be?
If you realized the power of
your imagination and creativity?
If you cherished silent abundance?
If you loved with all your heart,
not just somebody, but everybody?
If you dropped expectations and embraced the moment?

I wonder...
If the child in you played more each day?
If you realized human time is finite,
but your essence is infinite?
If each good deed healed the world and your being?
If wars ceased and peace prevailed?
If healthcare started at the root?
If every child, every senior,
had a healthy smile and someone to talk to?
With a program of personal responsibility,
learning ancient and modern lessons?
If every tear turned to gladness and self-worth?
If everyone learned to meditate,
to breathe well, to wake up a little more?
If teachers, doctors, lawyers, and all taught universal
empowerment, loving kindness, and encouragement?
If music, art, sports, and hobbies encouraged
love in thought, feeling, action?
If wisdom of differences inspired us all,
regardless of colour or background?
If "what if" thinking ceased, and "what is now"
changed habits for the better?
If your hunger was lovingly fed?
If you gathered tools to work towards goals,
while life lived you?
If you gave more to family, friends,
and yourself, for soul's light?
If every day began with a prayer of peace and gratitude?
If we shared our gifts, our love, our empathy,
without expectation, just because we can?

Angel

Angel, are you listening?
Human angel, messenger of love,
Lead with the grace of a dove,
While your feet stay grounded.
Move towards a deeper understanding,
Of love's boundless capacity.
It guides you through each lesson,
Love's vastness, both universal and personal,
Inspiring us to move, to nourish our bodies,
To rest, to savour our pace.
Shine your life, let your smile illuminate,
A spacious sense within, without.
Oh angel, you are light,
There is no doubt.
Angel, share your light and fly,
Feet on the ground, grounded within.
Touch your soul, touch each soul,
Touch the sky, expand your spirit.
Humanity's instinctive spirit,
Messenger who will never fade.
Peace places you in God's eye,
The wisdom of the present,
Every moment a wonder.
Oh angel, embraced by love,
No limits in this realm.
With eyes or hands, we give and embrace,
We smooth the rough edges.
Angel, know that you are enough.

World Peace

World peace will happen
When the light in every heart
Sparks a fierce yearning for harmony,
For the gentle touch of peace.

As world peace begins, we search,
and uproot every habit, every doctrine
that plants seeds
of hate,
of violence,
that demands the extinction
of people
just for existing.

When the veil of lies is lifted,
love takes root,
Healing begins and blooms into a vast tree,
its branches reaching toward the sky.

Wherever evil and darkness hide,
send light,
send prayer,
send love.

Oh Israel, Oh Israel

Oh Israel, oh Israel, Homeland of my people,
I have come to see the sunrise and the day.
I have come to hear the voices of this land,
To listen to the music of its souls.

Oh Israel, oh Israel, Homeland of my people,
I have come to witness the sunset and the dawn.
Wherever we are in the world,
We are one human family.

Through wars and peaceful journeys,
I have heard my soul.
Through battles and quiet moments,
I have felt the beating of my heart.
Oh Israel, oh Israel, Homeland of my people,
We are here and we will always be.

Wherever we are in the world,
we are one human family.
Adonai echad… God is one,
Ushmoh echad… God's voice is one,
Am Yisrael chai! Adonai echad,
ushmoh echad, Am Yisrael chai!

The laws of Noah,
the commandments, rules to live by for all,
Guiding us to peace and love,
To unity and respect.
Gratitude to the First Nations,
teachers of respect and love,
healing and wholeness.
Gratitude to humanity.

To every way of life that values peace,
Diversity, and the truth of understanding.

Let us examine our ways:
Open to our fullest potential,
Stay grounded, express love,
Own our emotions,
Rebalance to love's call for peace.

As is said in Jewish prayer for world peace,
"Then every nation
shall not have
war anymore."
Amen.

Chasia's Enchantment

Caring hearts, the abstract senses
intuition's invitation to all that is.
The six-star nations.

Oh my God and Oh my soul.
Infinite and in control.
And letting go, abundance rises,
and all that is discerned with love.

Sudden fulfillment of desire.
Curiosity, feeling flame and feeling fire.
Feeling whole, and doing this
in pure enchanted, abled bliss.

The more soul connected that we are,
it's written in a wind, a star,
and so I say imagine dreams,
imagine visions, smile and play
The infinite of every day.

Chasia's Enchantment

The Many Masks

The many masks that we present
in times of love and love's descent
are mirrored in a pool of light
that serves our journey day and night.

The light of all that ever was.
The light of all that is
is never lost in time and space.
We each receive with granted grace,
the perfect light of love divine
unmasking truth moves Earth and time.

The stance is yours, the stance is mine.
The endless possibility of every opportunity
is never lost in time or space.
We each receive with granted grace
the perfect act of love divine.

The stance is yours, the stance is mine,
this wave of rhythm, movement, gesture.
Environmental roots of Master,
Mistress of this universe,
Shakti, Shekhinah
no need at all to just rehearse.
We only need to look and see, you are that, it's true,
you're you. It's true I'm me
together in this family. Diversified humanity.

We belong to earth and sky.
How we breathe is how we fly.
Fly to wellness, fly to peace, letting go of all unease.
Gratitude, appreciation, patience, practice.
You will find delicious bliss and satisfaction,
the many masks unmasked in time.
Oh the living, so divine.
Wild wonder, you amazing child of this universe.
Ever being, every beginning,
in the endlessness of being.
We all have come a long way.
Children. Our inner child. Always with us.
No matter what we have experienced,
we can gently feel it step by step
and still remain in love with authentic being.
For this is truly love.

The decorations of life have been fun
but we know that the unity that arises
to authentic love was, is,
and always will be our birthright.
Our journeys are divine inspirations.

May we continue to let go of that
which does not serve us anymore.
Embrace, embody all that does.
May it grow and grow, lovingly, intentionally.

Sprinkle Joy

Sprinkle joy,
peace increases.
Sprinkle joy
everywhere and in your sleep.
We could all use joy's sweet release.
With love in every molecule
Sprinkle joy
through thoughts with ease.
Surrender to joy's endless lease.
Yes, sprinkle, sprinkle, sprinkle joy.
Sprinkle joy as
much as you please.
Imagine joy
in fantasies and in the real
at every meal.
Sprinkle joy, sprinkle joy,
may joy, like this friend, never cease.

Agni, The Fire

The *agni* fire of soul ignites the flame
that controls all roles and helps us see
the *sattva* purity of you and me.
To end *samskara*, memory of habit's wheel
without reflection might conceal
the *satya* truth to help us heal.
Like you and me, my friend, this fire glows,
inspired by life's yes's and no's.
The *agni* that fuels wellness thrives.
The *agni* of too much diminishes lives.
Anger, hunger, ego's grip
in groundless action, mind and lip.
Tamed and truthful to express
life's real passion, I confess.
How *agni's* fire passions life
so filled with guidance, lose the strife.
Feel the warmth of fire's flame
no overheating for there's no gain.
Contain life's fire to stay ignited
fueled with vision, stay delighted.
Attune, discern, unite
the empire of your gentle might.
Please your body, spirit, brain
and we can live a soul-filled plane.
Digesting food and feeling well.
Lightness of being, happiness in every cell.
Agni, the digestive fire of life.

Compass for the Lost

Words are a landscape, shifting,
Gestures are the wind that moves them.
Inside, outside, the art of connection
Is a fragile ecosystem.

Mindfulness, heart-driven,
Eyes that see through the haze.
Deceptions hide in plain sight, disguised as truth.

Why do we trust imposters?
Morality, dignity—
dormant seeds in the soil of belief,
Watered by lies. Desire clouds judgment,
Turns us away from caution.
We fall for stories, blind to the hidden snares.

Intuition whispered, but I chose to ignore.
Lessons learned through scars,
The anatomy of deceit.
Attention sharpens, intention guides,
A compass for the lost.
Communication, an art that starts within.

We are sheep in a labyrinth,
Paths pre-determined, yet malleable.
Rituals carve out clarity, courses redirect our steps.
Breathe with the earth, let life flow through,
still the chaos, find peace in the quiet.
Nature, music, solitude— Escape the urban clamour.
Tears cleanse, calm follows the storm.

Beauty is ephemeral,
Good counsel, a rare gem.
Inner voices, ancestral echoes,
guide us through the noise.
We are multifaceted beings,
Artists, teachers, healers,
Family of humanity, mothers, grandmothers,
Unified in our diversity, divinity.

Realign, shift perspective,
Listen beyond the words.
We own our voices, responsible for the
ripples they create.
Respect breeds clarity,
Conflict avoided through wisdom.
Evolved souls, masters of silent truths.

"Yum" or "yuck"— Simple filters for complex worlds.
Choose wisely, for communication is an art,
an enduring legacy.
Hope lives in each breath, words carry it forward.
Teach the next to love,
To speak with hearts unveiled.
We are children of the source,
AI, a tool—wield it well.
Let it refine, not replace,
The essence of our humanity.

Artful communication,
A bridge in a divided world.
Free to speak, to be, to weave the narrative anew.

Understand

When the teachings of hate,
passed through generations,
From misguided enemies
and all who hate blindly,
Or out of fear and clouded vision,
are overcome
By the clear light of truth,
shifting humanity
From hate to hope,
from lies to living truth,
From rigid beliefs
to raw facts and feelings,
Then our minds might
build mountains of love,

Valleys of life, healing, and wholeness.
The path from war to peace is winding and steep,
Yet these complexities can be gently untangled,
Through the quiet work of illuminating each other,
Heart to heart, emotionally, physically, spiritually.

Let us pray, love,
and send light to all nations,
Beginning with the wars
inside our own souls.
Meditate on love, meditate on peace,
act with love,
Act with peace, flee from darkness, turn to light.

The Divine spark of kindness and possibility
That is truly you, for your sake, for your family,
For the survival and flourishing of humanity.
From my soul to yours in this vast universe,
Understand that peace is but a breath away
If we will it with intention, attention, loving action.

We owe it
to the gift of life we all share.
Unconditional love
is your true essence,
your core,
Beneath layers of conditioning,
a unified consciousness,
Unconditional love
for yourself and all others.

Understand that world peace
begins in every heart,
Through life's karma,
embracing and shedding light,
Glowing light
into dark ideologies
and actions,
Transforming them
into real solutions for peace,
In each heart and soul,
in this world of nations.

Transformations: Interiors

What do you see when you look at me?
My angel wings? The dark? The light?
The bright? The dim?
What do you see when you look at me?

Butterfly rising, heart on the floor,
open and sharing, receding once more.
The depth of my being like yours
is concealed.
And all those who love us,
Help us reveal … the God spark,
divine spark of life and of being.
Opening up to what needs to be healed
to wholeness and all that in time
is revealed.
Oh, interiors. The vastness of nature
and nature within our Godly souls and being.

Open your eyes, breathe and make space
to feel all of the presence, so blissfully freeing.
Interiors.

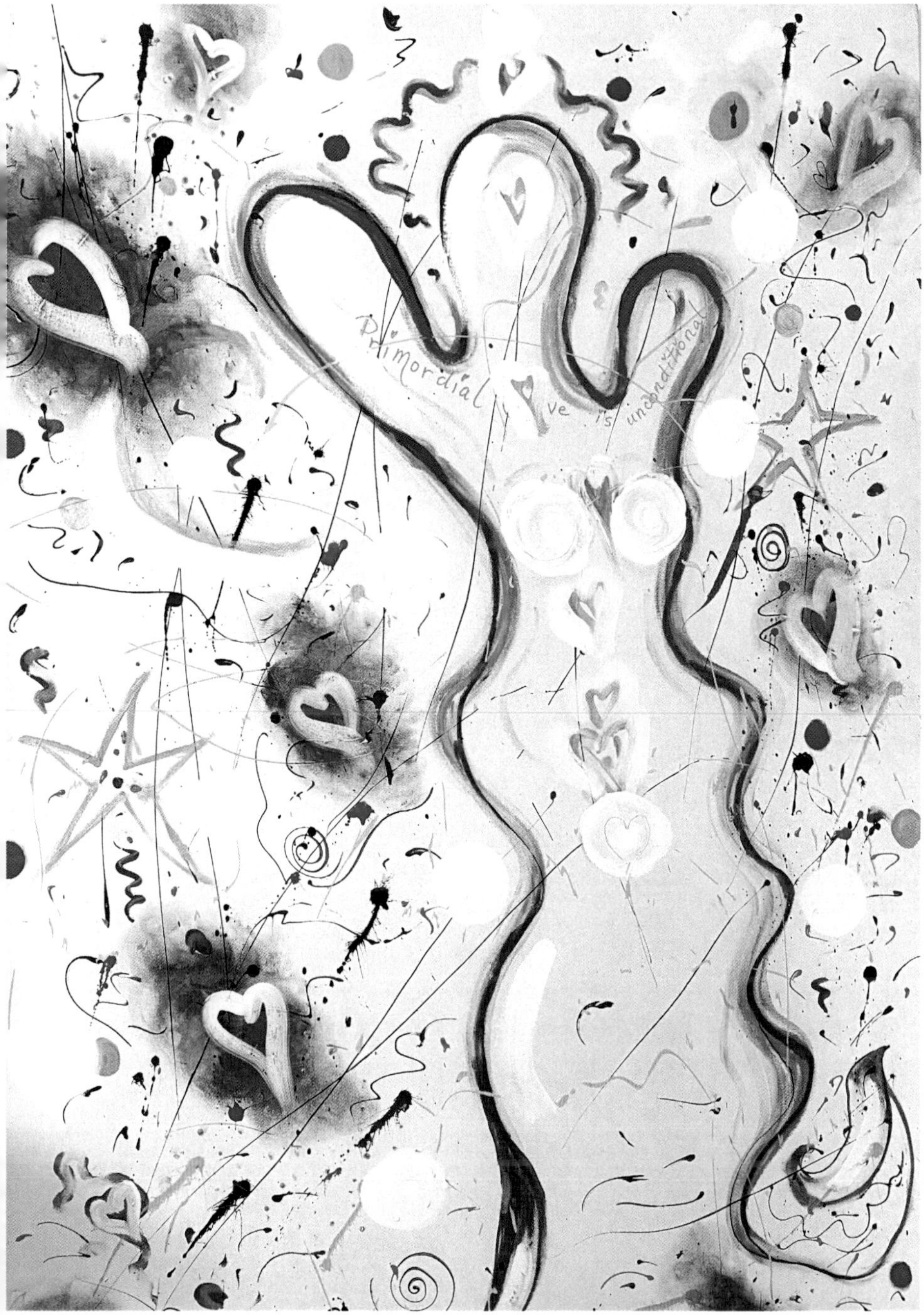

Transformations: Interiors

Kabbalah

Vessels
A divine light of creation shines in everyone.
Let it shine on wisdom, experiences, in all time.
Then understanding takes its shape
when wisdom and understanding unite
creating compassion in this world.

Grace awakens with compassion.
Love and moral code, the will that teaches humanity
to not be blinded materially.
We detach, we feel no lack when grace,
compassion lived unite.
They build another gift indeed.
The mercy that we need.

Above the splendour of all consciousness
exists the point of your fine being,
knowingness in the beauty,
the true beauty of bountiful seeing.

We witness our desires, expressing feelings here.
Victory aligning them with humble grandeur
and majesty of thoughts.
God's insights into Being,
choose what serves life at best.

Resonate with life's divinity
Love fully, God's request.
The active power, God's universal frequencies,
physical, sensual, intimate, spiritual.
Pouring divine and human worlds, all soaring.
Righteous deeds fulfill this world.

Creator's presence, opportunities, leads,
life's invitation to fill our needs.
Yes, our body and our earthly senses,
Our planet, the root of the tree.
The Holy Shekhina, the presence, the lower
unites with the upper. Both count, infinitely.
Original error caused separation,
we connect, repair and reground.
Becoming aware of all we can be and
all we can share and we're found.
The Kabbalah, in all four worlds:

Archetypal—*Atzilut*
Creative—*Briah*
Formative—*Yetsirah*
Material—*Assiah*

Shalom

One Life

You have one life to live.
Will you choose loving,
compassionate acts of kindness?
Seeking truth, fostering non-judgment, staying curious?
Treading the path of prayer, meditation, and actions for peace?

Live intelligently, gratefully, stand tall for others,
Battle the tides of biased propaganda.
When words infiltrate your mind, question them,
"Is this true? Is this truly true?"

Serve love, serve all lives with dignity.
Never again means never again.

Rise each morning with intent, act from love, live in peace,
watch your heart and soul thaw.
Be humbly grateful for a new day,
brimming with infinite possibilities.

Ask yourself, "Who am I?"
Exhale all that does not serve
your tender, strong, loving heart.

One life to live with dignity, balance,
share your love for all you feel and all you'll heal.

Laugh richly, live entirely.
Whatever you believe, believe this:
You are more than enough, my friend,
A well of potential.
Pour all you have into love in this one life.

Torah

The golden rays on Moses' crown,
as he who holds the tablets in his arms.
The Ten Commandments containing
the six hundred thirteen mitzvot, ten ethical rules for
living and loving in holiness through life for all life.

The Jews are the Nation that were given the Torah
and the Torah brings the light of
the Torah wisdom into the world
for the world, for the love of humankind
and the awe of the divine one God
who created the world in six days
and rested on the seventh.

The golden light of divine glory, rules for living
and being through Torah, trickles down into every
human's story. Torah! Torah! Torah!

All that has been created in this universe can
be found and is still unfolding from Torah,
the teachings, almost six thousand years old.

The written law came after the oral law and the
written law has been with us for almost four thousand
years. May that which imbues every heart and soul
with glorious life keep unfolding.
And if you choose, learn a little Torah.

Torah. For one and all.

Life Lesson

Inwardly and outward free.
Compassion, laughter, trust emerge
in the choice of rising courage.
Mind, brain, and heart unite impart
the knowingness of answers you will find.
Torah's hidden messages trusting time
to reveal all that makes you love and heal.
Sharing timely what you feel.
Develop calmness, restful mind.

The power of our authenticity
lifts spirit, sense of being.
Remember all the storms of life subdued
simply with a shift of mood.
Vedic words *Satya,* truth; *Prema* love
blending energies above.
Kehttehr, crown,
unification's call.
Tifereht, beauty of it all,
and below to now bestow.
Malchut, foundation deep,
life's learning, oh the letting go.

Delight in all that you do know
deep inside inspires so.
Wisdom *chokhmah*, to clarify the choice
of divine love and love's voice.

Laws and attributes to heal.
Hear the call to rise and be.
Hear this call, calm naturally.
Inwardly and outward free.

Tu Bishvat
the Fifteenth of Shvat

Happy Birthday trees,
Oh Happy New Year trees.
The rain of life has mostly ceased.
The trees begin a brand new lease
of growing buds into soft leaves and
fruits of nature, as breezes tease
and bounty meets our hearts with joy.
The trees' New Year on Tu Bishvat
Renews the hope of all we've got
to so inspire our desire, universally
to grow and stretch and truly be
as supple as a growing tree.

In Israel and in the world
to share the buds of love most fruitfully
take care of trees,
take care of all, in nature and in life.

With gratitude to God divine,
Creator's world, we share the work
and harvest the whole plentitude
of every bowl of food.
In time, in blessing.
Food for body, mind and spirit.
Raise your voice, good day, let's hear it.
Tu Bishvat's a happy time
with thankfulness to the divine.

Yoga

Yesterday today and tomorrow
is open to embrace. Gurus, sages all agree
the value of yoga philosophy.
Stretch mind and body greatly
with postures right for you.

Meditate to elevate your internal grounding
and de-stress with ease
in the practice of yoga every day, if you please.
As we work with our bodies, our minds grow in flow.
We may learn to listen more wisely
to the yes and no of our habits
and our rituals that bring much more
joy, peace and balance to our lives each day.
Our hearts rise in union in a well lived way.
Ancient wisdom brings gentle teachings
for the world to embrace.

Yoga lessons for the present,
karmic teaching in play.
Each yoga pose has a message
for your life and soul be open mainly
for the inspiration of your truth as it unfolds.
Yoga lessons work so well for the aging and the youth
the sacred, the divine, the bliss of human being
in the natural that resonates in breath
and breath's own time!

Namaste, an ancient way to healthy stay.

I Breathe In

I breathe. I breathe in love and life and yes, I let go of what does not serve serenity. I trust, I love, I am wholeness. Forevermore. I breathe in love and I breathe out whatever does not serve peace. I breathe in stillness, and I breathe out chaos. I breathe in opening, and I breathe out constriction. I breathe in possibility, I breathe out resistance. I breathe in joy, I breathe out lack of joy. I breathe in strength, I breathe out fear. I breathe in healing, I breathe out hurt. I breathe in Torah, I breathe out worry. I breathe in Kabbalah, I breathe out ignorance. I breathe in yoga, I breathe out senselessness. I breathe in sutras, I breathe out confusion. I breathe in Upanishads, I breathe in understanding, I breathe in the bodhi tree, I breathe out selfishness. I breathe in all teachings of all the ways of life that support life. I breathe out falsehoods. I breathe in love, I breathe out love. I breathe in support, communication, I breathe out love, creativity and forgiveness. I breathe in prosperity. I trust, I love, I am wholeness, just like you, forevermore.

Mantra

Mantra.
Vehicle of the mind.
Spaciousness.
Heart's desire.
Illuminated white sun.
Oh, the planets and the surrender
to all that makes life
a meditation.

The sweet sounds manifested
from the unmanifested.
Primordial sounds.
Sounds of nature
And your own
heart beating
mantra.

Mantra

Soul to Self

Do not be afraid to keep stepping into the truth
of all you are. Remember to refine
your spirit, mind, and body's gifts.
Grounded in your presence.

Receive and share your individual treasures.
Your happiness, your laughter, your insight.
Your awareness, your beauty, your intuition, your focus,
your credibility, creativity and wholeness.
Express your passion, your purpose and
connect to your connection
as you continue to unfold, exquisitely
in silence, observation, or expression in life.

Your magnificence shines through your loving,
growing self-esteem.
True confidence and the surrender to your healed
and healer's gifts within you.
You are an artist of your own life.
Voicing your truth with dignity, grace.

Wild wonder, you amazing child of this universe.
Ever being, ever beginning,
in the endlessness of being.
We all have come a long way.
Children. Our inner child. Always with us.
No matter what we have experienced,
we can gently feel it step by step
and still remain in love with authentic being.
For this is truly love.

The decorations of life have been fun
but we know that the unity that arises in
our authentic love was, is,
and always will be our birthright.
Our journeys are divine inspirations.

May we continue to let go of that
which does not serve us anymore.
And embrace, embody all that does.
May it grow and grow, lovingly, intentionally.

No Hatred

No hatred can overpower the longing for peace
That resides deep within our hearts.
Every child must rise from the chaos,
Breaking free from the web of evil.
We are all children,
Yearning for the gentle touch of unity.
With spirits and bodies intertwined,
We need open minds
And hearts that seek balance.
No hatred, no demoralization.
Be mindful of our teachings,
Our words, our actions.

Lift up and support those in need of kindness.
Do not incite conflict or blame those who defend
Their home and loved ones.
Wounds of the mind, body, and spirit
Shatter human dignity.
Never let displaced anger
Suppress the divine spark within.
Born of love, both divine and human,
Our world thirsts for it. Please, no hatred.
Awaken your primal love,
Choose to live, love, and heal.

Embrace the wholeness of who you truly are,
Of who we all are. When we choose the right path,
Time and again, after every conflict and war,
Supporting, rehabilitating, allowing time to grieve,

To grow, to learn trust, and to live fully.
Help heal others, declare "Never Again"
To blatant hatred, to those who seek destruction.
Let everyone learn the path to peace.
There is no peace
In the agenda of destruction.

This is why,
Long before her return to ancient, sacred lands,
She and her people,
Few in number,
But vast in contributions,
Stand for the oppressed.
Strong with many, from varied ways of life,
Faiths, and paths.

Is she perfect? No,
Like all nations, she is not.
Do her people
Deserve peace, to address their needs?
Yes, absolutely!
Her people, like many,
Pray for global peace.
May we live without hatred,
As we journey through life,
Learning greater humanity,
Love, balance, peace within and without.
For a life grounded in love, peace,
And the sacred spirit in us all.

Power of Hope

Remember, the power of hope is real.
Childhood innocence that
ignites ego-less states,
removes judgment and criticism.

Lighthearted, carefree.
Play a little each day.
Accept people in the best light.
We all have our burdens.

We all are looking for solutions at times.
Sit, relax, refrain from criticizing
yourself or anybody else.
Notice, observe, let go.
People will notice you are more welcoming,
for lightheartedness is the heart of freshness.
And then hope is ready to be renewed.
We are potential, pure potential, not of what is
but all that might be.

Our potential for limitless awareness
overcomes all limitations.
Remember the power of hope is real.

River of Life

Forever the river of life just flows.
It turns a bend and goes and goes.
The surface changes with the mood,
calm or raging filled with food,
the oxygen of life in flow.
The river bed, unknown and known.
The rocks and shorelines, mud and sand.
The rain and sleet, the snowy land.

The stars shine down, moon's face and sun.
The river flows and says,

"Just come to fill your lungs
with nature's bliss."

And there you stand and here it is,

"Be playful, clear each day."

Anchored Play

Anchored, I can play and never drift away.
But let my soul rise and let it flow,
into the stream of life's own show.
For in the play of life I see
the very real of fantasy
brought down to Earth, the vision seen
and practical made of the dream.

Focus, intention, attention, and will.
And destiny reveals itself,
Oh, the joy of anchored play.
For life says, "Play with surprise and purpose!
Come my way."

And in discernment, I can find
the affluence and openness that
guides my being and my mind.
The knowingness,
the flow of all eternal holiness,
anchored.
Once again life says,
"Come let's play."

Unified Spirituality and Truth

Study true Torah, Kabbalah deep codes.
Yogic and Vedic wisdom to awaken union.
Union of transits, true transits to life.
African healers, First Nations connections
are beings of light.
The Tao and Confucius are Asian and Eastern.
All of this is learning and sharing.

The Inca, the Celtic, the Toltec, the North.
The wise ones of all lives, truth knowers, deep truth.
Together we join sharing planet and space.
To repair and heal this world with
love and with grace.

All sacred teachings—
The Christians, the Muslims, the Jews
over four billion Abrahamic people
all of the others, we all need some healing.
The great and the small, sharing lifeline and all
the world according to the Torah is one narrow bridge
may we all hold hands spiritually in love
sharing this earth.

Shalom. Om. Namaste, Salam

Mindfulness

Our heart eyes feel and see and we respond.
The eyes on our face just might deceive us
but not our heart eyes.

Our heart is the gateway to our spirit.
It is our soul that our heart
opens up the door to.
Our heart and our heart's eyes are
the gateway to our soul
that frees our spirit
into right action, always.

The purity that is our whole
welcomes us just as we are,
complete in the frequency and resonance
of *Chesed*, loving kindness to our true self,
children of God, in the mystery of life.

Let us surrender blissfully to this mindful practice
with attention to every moment
with our heart eyes' intention
helping to will our destiny.

The Honey-Sweet Torah

Honey sweet is the enjoyment,
the learning that Torah teaching brings
to every child, to every soul.
God gave the Jews the responsibility and joy to learn,
to teach to share the Torah teachings with all from
generation to generation.

Torah knowledge, faith in action, that's the call.
Mitzvot good deeds, commandments,
life's ups and downs, and turn arounds
happen on this plane.
Torah teaching help to keep
the world in love, and sane.
Tempered feelings, wisdom shows, how respect
just grows and grows.

The word is power when explained.
Anger, hurt, can all be tamed.
Righteous actions can be named.
We're only human, stop all blame.
Turn to wisdom teachings flame.
Flame of honest feelings touched.
Dare to question, welcome much.

Kabbalah is within this learning.
Books and books of understanding.
Rabbis spending lifetimes to bring clarity
to you and me through the teachings of Torah
and Kabbalah in practical spirituality lived.

Guided lessons teach us how
to stand in spirit tall.
Love for God and love for elevating life
from the mundane into the sacred.
Love for humanity, ethics and taking care of the
natural world that God created.
Using intelligence and heart
for the good of humankind
with exploration and
loving awareness revealed in its lessons.

Be Kind

Respect the omnipresent and you will acquire
an inspired passion for life.
With a foundation of openness,
one gains insight into the reasons
for the cycles of life.

From purity arises a deep desire
to protect one's body.
And from the purification of one's essence,
cheerfulness arises.
And with it, one pointed concentration,
mastery of our senses
and the capacity for sustaining
the vision of our true self.

The innocence and knowing,
the pure potential,
and the grace of embodied acceptance.
From contentment,
one gains deep supreme happiness.
Be kind to yourself,
be kind to others, body, mind and spirit.

This Much We Know

This much we know, that no matter how much
we know there is more to know, to understand,
to transcend to move to perfect peace.
Within ourselves, within our wondrous worlds of
blessings, healings and wholeness.

This much we know, that with every day and every night
a new beginning comes as we live here on planet Earth.

Whatever brings us just a little closer to finding answers
to our questions fills the gaps of misunderstandings into
profound honouring of each other's journey
in time, space and beyond.
This much we know, love's and life's potential
lives here in our every breath. This much we know.

We Are Coming Together

God alone gives me peace of mind.
Of course you are in my heart all life long.
Oh my dear God, you are in my heart.
Each breath says,
"I am here with you."
All the people I know are here with you.
God alone, God alone gives me peace of mind.
I am happy, I am filled with love from God.
This was how the world was built.
In every soul, a spark of God alone.
We are coming together from God alone.

Matrix of Love

Every connection, every direction,
every selection of thought,
feeling,
emotion,
in the spaciousness
of love's coherence
guides us into the mystery,
into the magnitude
of the matrix.

Open yourself up.
Dare to be
in the matrix
of love's equanimity.

Oh, the matrix of love, of life,
of seeing, of feeling,
of touching, of sensing, of being
in the matrix of love.

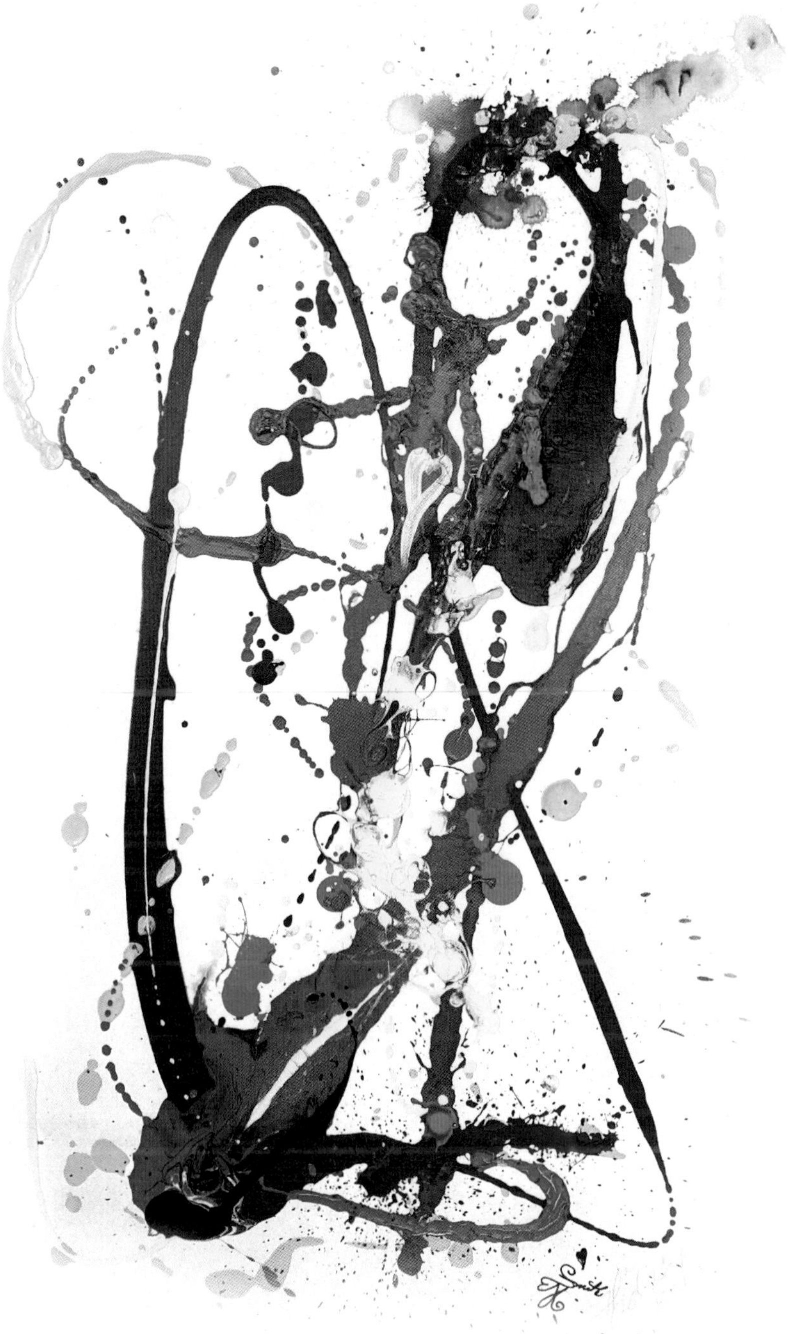

Matrix of Love

Home to You

In spite of any sorrow or heartache, we have held,
released, we find tomorrow a world all by itself.
Unfolding in each moment
the hope, the joy, the bliss
of everything before us
one moment at a time.

How can anybody miss the opportunities
awaiting each person on this Earth
to grow in their own story?
Each moment like a bird, a possibility unfolding.
The air upon your skin, the sunlight changing.

Every moment in the world we're in,
the beauty that's within you
could never cease to call upon the moment
that is new in every moment.

See the shawl of love and beauty
through tear-stained pillows, cries.
Wash your face, sweet darling, and empty to surprise
the incoming wisdom, the joy of who you are.
No matter what the problem
solutions are not far.
The dignity of your own heart
will bring you home to you.

Life Talk

The lustrous beam of light I see
connects the all of you and me.
We're born into a time and place,
applaud and cheer and land and praise
the miracle of life and living,
circulating lambent giving.

Nature, God, art, science, space.
Common sense, resplendent face.
Imagination may reveal
the affluence that you conceal.

Ideas, hopes and inspiration
for the world, for every nation.
Vociferate with confidence,
uniquely you, do take a chance.

Amplify the call to love
the olive branch, the snow white dove.
Resources, we have got enough
to mine the field of heart.
That beam of light, a grand unveiling.
That's the way to start.

Prasanta Aloka
Peaceful Brilliance

Prasanta aloka, peaceful brilliance.
I invite divinity, God, Creator
to flow and flood my being
With peaceful brilliance.

OM

Living Passion

Cultivate joy, sharing what excites you.
Discover what ignites your passion.
Discover your true purpose.
Everyone has dharma, a special purpose in this life.
We all have unique gifts, we have unique needs.
Connecting with our dharma
allows us to express them.
What do you really, really want
and what do you really, really need?
How will you use your unique gifts and talents
to serve yourself and others?
One way to find out is to explore, try new things.
Let go of what doesn't serve you anymore.
And stay open to love, to life, to joy,
to whatever inspires you.
Living passion.

Life Poem

Choose to live each day midst life's
tears and woes and trials.
You will feel love's buoyancy uplifting you.
To yourself be fair and kind, and
to others you will find
that blood is flowing in your skin,
everyone is truly kin.

Bless and give by how you live.
Gentleness is strength you know.
May love guide you as you walk
endlessly in every talk
that brings through silence radiance,
the soulful whisper of this dance.
The simple things that so enhance our journey.
Oh the realms of love's own ranges.
Laugh, cry, love, and truly be.
Touch truth and then set it free.
Whatever it is, you are in the tree of life.

Exercise your loving ways.
Express your love exquisitely.
Embraceable and loveable
no matter what has happened.
Dare to dream to visualize, to sparkle
with sincerity. Step into your reality, now.
Patience, practice, real, no dress rehearsal.
Simply be. Express yourself and you will see.
In each day, most naturally.
The you you are, that shining star.

My Heart in My Hand

My heart in my hand.
A kiss of desire.
Grounded in restful awareness.
I feel warmth of fire
igniting the *agni*, within me, this fire.

I feel my soul rising higher and higher.
Oh, infinite truth, infinite flow.
Who knows where imagination will go?
What will reveal itself in creative exposure.

In rising, fulfillment, enlightened awareness
Oh, do we dare to just be and to see
where life's road will take us?
Yes, you and me.
All of us
in this incredible dream.
My heart in my hand, enchantedly.

My Heart in My Hand

Love Comforts

Translation of Liebeh Traist

There comes a time
when love knows
what heart must learn.
Love comforts everyone.
Soul! Body! Mind! Spirit!
Not much needed.
Heart will hear a drop of love
just like the sun shines light,
a drop of love lights everyone,
and everywhere, for love is true.
Honey deep, magic, bliss is love's pure kiss.
Sweet and precious, love's own fire.
There comes a time when love does know
what heart must learn.
Love comforts!
Love inspires!

Liebeh Traist

Ess koomt a tzeit ven leibeh vaist
vohs hartz mooz lehrnen
leibe traists alehmehn!
neshomeh! goof! mayukh! ruakh!
neesht a sukh gedarfn
hartz veht hehrn, a trop foon leibeh
poonkt vee dee zoon shynt leekht
a trop foon leibeh buhlikhts alehmehn.
oon oomehtoom, vyl leibeh eez troi
honik teef,keeshehf grestehr gleek
eez leibeh's tzeertlekh keesh
zees oon tyehr, leibeh's aign fyehr
Ess koompt a tseit ven Leibeh vaist
vohs hartz mooz lernehn
Leibeh traist! Leibeh buhgystehrt!
Leibeh traist.

Our Window to Hope

Our window to hope
Lies waiting in our hearts,
With self-love and universality.
Golden rays of light
In every conscious breath.

Hope, love, and peace greet us,
Compassion and respect for all others,
Annihilates anger and incivility.
Stay curious. Curious to what you hear,
Use your moral compass to see, react, respond.

Breathe in lightness of being.
Breathe out precious lightness.
All precious possibilities
To find love within.
Live with empathy. Live with sincerity.
Pay attention to your intentions.

Grow grandly, live in peace with yourself,
And with all others, as much as possible.
In my imperfect wholeness,
Just like yours,
Create questions that reveal the cosmic divine.
The natural, undeniable answer is always love.

Beneath fears, hurts, angers, and misunderstandings,
Is the will to live harmoniously,
With ourselves and with all others.
We change the world when we change ourselves.

The art of divinity is within us,
Born of the celestial ether,
Of your sweet affection and need for connection.
Connection to yourself, to your soul,
Connection to your heart, to health, to joy.
To higher consciousness and on Earth.

With labours of love leading us,
Towards a sustainable world of beauty,
Guided by labours of love,
Towards a world of sustainable beauty,
The meek and the mighty support each other,
In love, peace, and unity, making decisions,
With inclusive diversity at their core.

Grace, and awe beyond our imaginations.
The meek, the mighty, supporting each other,
Love, peace, and unity, empowering decisions,
Of inclusive diversity.
This is our window to hope,
Realized in each breath.

Go! Go! Go! To Your Heart

Go to your heart and say,
"Ananda, Lev, teach me to love
more clearly, more deeply
by the light of all the space within me.
More space than I ever knew that I had."

Everyone has so much room
because what brought you into being
is invisible, untenable, and real.

Sound waves, atoms, molecules,
move and shape sound, touch, sight,
feelings, taste, insight, intuition,
clairvoyance, audio voyance,
extra-sensory perception.
Feelings travel in our bodies to other people.
The world herself was given to us with
signs and messages through energy fields
that we cannot see, and those we can.

Exploring the possibilities of logic,
you will find there are many things that happen
beautifully in this world that have no logic.
Love is a controlled, open freedom, happiness is an
elusive butterfly, but joy is love in action.
It is always available.

Happiness can bring joy, however, if happiness
is dependent upon anyone or anything, as most
happiness is, it is temporary.

When we feel sad or frustrated,
knowing we can feel whatever
we are truly feeling brings us joy, even in the
midst of whatever emotion is presenting itself.
There is an ecstatic stillness that is
the presence of that knowingness.
It will always bring us home.
It invites us to self-care and self-love always.
That kind of joy is a marvelous fit. Try it.
Allow your joyful memories to stay at the forefront
of your life the best you can, and the habit of
remembering them will bring you back to centre if
you get a little lost, as we all can.

Love is the answer always.
What is your question? Sit with it.
Listen to some relaxing instrumental music.
Sit with it.
Outside or inside your home,
or someplace you can mindfully see
The truth of the beauty that is you.

If that does not resonate with you,
be gentle on yourself.
Breathe, and know that life is there with you.
How do we know we are being breathed?
Who or what is breathing us?
That presence is always there.
We just forget to remember.
Go! Go! Go to your heart!

Eekh Sheek Deer a Koosh
I Send You a Kiss

Eekh sheek deer a koosh
I send you a kiss

meet leebeh oon een fryndshuhft
with love and in friendship.

doo beest azoi tyehr tsoo meer
You are so dear to me

Eekh sheek a sukh liebeh oif dem
veent glykh tzoo deer
I send you a lot of love on the wind, right to you

meet duhnkbehrshuhft glykh tzoo dyn teer
with thankfulness, right to your door.

Dee teer foon dyn hartz
The door of your heart

eekh zeh ohfn oon klohr
I see open and clear

ohngefeelt meet dyn hartzeekeit
filled with your heartfulness.

tahkeh frynd, yohr eebehr yohr
Really friend, year after year,

blyb gebehntcht oon blyb gezoont
stay blessed and stay healthy

meet shmaichlen oif dyneh leepn
with smiles on your lips.

Eekh sheek deer a koosh
meet leebeh oon een fryndshuhft
I send you a kiss
with love and in friendship

myn frynd
my friend,

mineh frynd
my friends,

myneh keendehr, myn fameelieh, myneh ainiklehkh
my children, my family, my grandchildren,

oon ahlleh mentchn een dehr velt!
and all the people in the world.

Meet leebeh, een fryndshuhft, myn frynd, myneh keendehr,
myn fameelieh, myneh ainiklehkh
oon ahlleh mentchn een deur velt! bleibt shehfehdeek
een neshomeh, hartzeek meet
hofenoong!
With love and in friendship, my friend,
my children, my family, my grandchildren,
and all the people in the world.
Stay abundant in soul, heartful with hope.

eech sheek deer a koosh
I send you a kiss.

Namaste, Shalom.

Kabbalah Insights

The wisdom, and the beauty, and the deep lessons
of Kabbalah are teachings that are referred to as
The Tree of Life.
Ten utterances, it is said in Judaic study,
created the universe.
It is that what God, Adonai, created.

Kehtehr. A divine light of creation
shines in everyone, and on everyone.
Chochmah. Let it shine on wisdom,
experiences in time.
Binah. Then understanding takes its shape
when wisdom and understanding unite
in creating the world. Gentleness arrives.
Chesed. Grace awakens compassion.
Loving kindness. Love, the moral code.
Gevurah. The love that teaches humanity
to not be blinded materially.

When grace, compassion lived unite,
they build another gift indeed.
The mercy that we need, above the
splendour of all consciousness, *Tiferet* exists.
This is the point of your being — knowingness
in the beauty, true beauty of bountiful seeing.

Netzach. Witness our desires expressing feelings here.
Victory aligning them, experiences dear.
Hod. Grandeur, the majesty of thoughts,
God's insight to our vision. Our choosing what serves
best, life, and life's request.
Yesod. The act of power of God's
universal frequencies, a physical, intimate,
spiritual pairing of divine and human worlds,
all sharing. Righteous deeds fulfill the world,
as creators deeds present
opportunities to fill our needs.
Yes, our body and earthly senses,
our planet, the root of the tree.

Malchut, the presence, the lower unites
with the upper, both count.
Original error, cost separation.
We connect, and we repair, and
we ground true awareness.
We are aware of all we can be,
and all we can share
through the Tree of Life
and the Teachings of Kabbalah.

Shalom, my friends.

Being

Being in our being, we can recognize ourselves
in each other's reflection.
Needing to love unconditionally
and needing to be loved unconditionally.
As beings of brilliance in the phenomenal field
of un-mined greatness, humility,
in the splendour of our world here we are.
Being. This is a gift imbued by energy
Which creates universes, the divine energy
that fashions every aspect of life.

We exist in this miraculous world, together.
We have come into life to develop,
to share new stories and to
honour our ancestors.

Remember to learn from history.
Imagine new vistas out of the innocence,
compassion, intelligence, intuition, flexibility,
joy, beauty, healing, and transformation.
Yes, honouring the past and
looking into each moment
As we move into the future.

This liberation of transforming transcends.
We attend to our own being.
Being in our being and in so doing helping
all other beings.

Promise of the Ocean Song

The ocean song within you,
that fills your every pore.
Just close your ears and listen,
you'll be right there I'm sure.
Find it. Breathe consciously.
Pranayama within you.

For life created ocean and life created you,
so don't forget the motion
there's nothing you can't do
that's meant in life for you.

Rejoice in using knowledge
and feelings to expound
the wealth of life around you.
Let go and you'll have found
silly somethings happening
that might get in the way
of you and your true mission.
Learn and love each day.

By caring deeply for yourself
and all you see and know,
your spirit will embrace you.
Your radiance will glow.

The ocean song within you will grow a rhythm true
And carry you across the waves
Till you come home to you.

Embodiment

Our bodies hold so many feelings,
sometimes we don't know we're concealing.
Experiences, tucked away, and then they rise,
What do you say? What's best to do?
Acknowledge what is going on in you.
Name an emotion, a thought-rising feeling.

And if you do not know, be gentle with yourself.
Find someone you can talk to.
Go for a walk.
Allow yourself to be, embody your healing.

Embodied feelings need to integrate
and sometimes you need
someone else to listen.

Then you'll open insightfully
and see the steps to take rightfully.
Embodied self, make no mistake.
We all have places we could go into our history.
and when there is something that is blocked,
revealing truth, embracing love may truly help
to uncover mystery.

How you show up really counts.
Be loving to yourself.
Embodiment of who you are
requires your embracement of the you
that you let go,
that needs to come back home.
The spirit of your being saying,
"Focus. Do not roam."

Experience is showing you
one of many ways embodied
truth frees you from the haze.
Be free in who you are.
Embodied peace. Embodied joy.
Embodied being.
Shine your star.

Music

I listen to the music of life.
I hear it in the rests.
In the full circle of life.
In the reminder of that red blood
running through my veins.
The blood within everyone
who is singing a song
of life.

Sunshine sprinkled everywhere
like leaves falling,
leaves growing,
the blue of sky and the waters,
and the gold and silver bounty
of all the elements.

Oh, the music of the mountains and the sea,
and the rivers, the oceans,
and the ever-green of love
in your heart, your body, your mind
and your spirit.

Illumination.
I hear the music
of life.
Listen carefully, joyfully
to the music of life, in each moment.

Music

Dear Soul

Our hearts are beating beautifully
because the divine allows.
Brains brighten when spaciousness enters
through stillness, through kindness,
through love, through compassion,
through common sense,
and through creativity.

We become the watcher of
our thoughts and feelings
and as we watch and observe,
we know this to be true—
The Light, the God spark,
the grand nature our spirit
within and around us is felt.
Our soul spirit communicates with us.
We only need to listen.
Our souls are the embodiment
of our Being.

Just Once

Just once you meet someone
and notice something. Just once.
A tilt of chin, a gait, a grin.
A shape of hand, or face.
A shoe, a coat, a posture stance
A generous smile, a pace.

Wide eyes, deep pools of light.
Raven hair, ginger, blond, brown, slender, thick.
How someone moves, the sound of voice.
The way they speak, or make a choice.
Their walking grace, humility.
Their dignity, civility.

A memory forever etched.
Just once you meet
someone
and notice
something.

In your heart, the memory
that makes you smile.

Imagination

Let our imaginations never cease to
create the stories
that imbue our life with meaning.
Creativity and knowing,
shedding as much light as we can
in each moment,
in each magnificent vibrating breath.

Be blessed in this, the knowingness
above, below, within,
reflected in each bless-ed divine soul.
May we all be vessels of purpose and unity
to all that supports a loving, meaningful life.

Let us take flight like a white dove,
blessing our families, our friends, community,
with all we have plenty of.
With this pure light of caring,
here's to our dreams come true
for a loving world, whole
abundant in full view,
where sound values help us live healthfully
adjusting to life and life's throng.

Generation to generation and all our life long.
Li'heetra-ot. Until we meet again.
May our imaginations never cease
to create more love and help bring more peace
to our own lives and all others.
Intelligence alive and well,
we're all sisters and all brothers.
Let our imaginations never cease
to bring out the best in each of us
and into the world.

Shalom. Namaste.

America

America, America,
the lotus blooms in you.
America, America,
butterfly dreams come true.
America, America
Shakhina,
America,
transforming with whatever is your prayer.

America, America.
Stay strong and blessed and true.
To everyone, America, that lives inside of you.
America, America,
may angels watch and see.
America, America,
your soul, inspired, free.
America, America,
the kundalini flame.
America, America,
meritocracy reclaim.

May every nation live in truth
Of teachings built of love.
America, America, the eagle and the dove.

Oh Canada

Oh Canada, Oh Canada,
hearts of passion rise.
Sunset, morning sunrise, before Canadian eyes
and all who live here.

People who have come to build
a home in this fine land.
A melting of so many hearts
who live to understand.

The Unity. Opportunity. Community.
Oh Canada, Oh Canada,
we stand saluting thee.
Oh Canada, Oh Canada,
a country living free.
Oh Canada, Oh Canada,
a wondrous country too.
May everyone who lives in Canada
bring pride and joy to you, Oh Canada.

Learning from the land we see
the forests and the mountains,
the lakes and streams and rivers.
The ocean and the cities and the towns

Oh Canada, Oh Canada,
forever strong and free.
With love and pure humility
compassion is the key.
Oh Canada.

To the Children Everywhere

To the children everywhere,
we understand your every care.
The world needs your creative flow,
a river of hope, heartfully abundant,
unbounded, untamed,
coursing through the landscapes of your dreams.

In all you do, you grow,
through choices, living true,
evolving lives, each step, each moment,
in work and play, in every way.

Travel, rest, research, invest,
be wise, no lies, embrace the quest.
You'll learn, you'll teach, your mind will feast,
on wonders of the world,
north, south, east and west.

Do be careful with what you do,
with what you see,
let kindness be your guide,
sincerity your creed.

Live freely, in love's intention,
with respect, moral in every dimension.
We count on you to teach us well,
youth united, stories swell.

Respecting all,
who knows what love and growth will tell?
Children, we are all,
it's true,
stretch and dream,
let your visions break through.

Connect each phase,
with all your might,
each failure, each success,
leads you to the light.

Whatever your journey holds,
embrace it tight,
for it will turn out
just right.

Live well, love well,
be well, today and every day.
Know that each day has its gifts,
be grateful, be thankful,
child of the universe.

Live, love, laugh, and simply be,
in the vast, infinite tapestry
of life's grand mystery.

Sacred Sensuality

Sacred sensuality, a reverie of
tenderness, adoration and love
leads to that which serves
remembrance of our bond to life.
Create rituals built out of love.

A bath to fill the senses and relax the body.
A steam or shower, flowing droplets of water.
Life's elixir, relaxing, refreshing,
invigorating the body,
and the mind follows.

Creams, lotions, oils, to gently
massage the body and say,
"I love you," to the gift of the body.
Sacred sensuality, spirit's way, sacred nature.

Sultry summer, inspired spring,
feeling autumn, wondrous winter.
Seasons of our lives in sacred sensuality.
One with the other, and in our solitude.
Sacred sensuality.

True Self Love

True self love is not selfish.
To care for our whole self,
every part of us is necessary to feel whole.

In nourishing and nurturing our mind
with knowledge,
wisdom,
creativity,
enlightenment,
in honouring our bodies
with
movement,
nourishment,
exercise,
intimacy,
sound and healthful touch,
in honouring our spirits
with nature,
precious
books,
stories and
shared love,
we live the selflessness of love
more ready to share it all in joy and gratitude.

True self-love reminds us of the other
as they are, but a reflection of us,
whole-fully.

Love's Flow, Body Knows

And body says, live with an illuminated heart
free from jealousy, resentment and anger.
Move into love's flow.

A heart that touches others simply, deeply, is yours.
Cultivate it, feed it with loving warmth,
gentleness in gestures, and expressions.

Allow yourself to fall in love again
with life in action and in silent reverie.
The greater cosmic blessing is operating
all the time, hidden and revealed
to body, mind and spirit.

Give love with ease and sincerity
and watch what happens.
Illuminate yourself and all others
with an awakened body,
an awakened heart of love.

In Between the Kisses

In between the kisses, soft and gentle.
Heartfelt, warming.
Our embracing, strong and soulful,
eyes meeting eyes, smiling gracefully
with affection and reflection
in each other's eyes and souls.
Breathing, bountiful and peaceful.
Radiantly, two hearts beating.
Love's assurance, in coherence
in between the kisses, soft and gentle.
Sacred bliss of this being,
in this love, this life, this all.

Sending Love in Being

Centred in our being, being with
our body, heart and mind.
Relaxed thoughts, relaxed body,
relaxed heart, relaxed mind.
We can feel, touch, sense, see
and hear the symphony of our being-ness.
Cosmic blessing, lived in peacefulness and love.
We have this love to give, emotionally,
physically, mentally, spiritually.
In sharing love appropriately,
centred in our being, we awaken.
Om, Shalom, Habrakha, the blessing.

Aleph

The Aleph, the first letter of the Jewish alphabet
brings all worlds together.
The Divine within all.

Aleph is the connector to all the worlds.
The world of possibility, the world of ideas
not yet laid out in a blueprint.
And the world of actual blueprint and design.
And this Earthly world of form.
All four worlds integrated.

All four worlds being lived at once.
Aleph. The heart of it all,
Aleph. The king and queen-liness of
the universe combined as one.
Aleph. Four worlds, like the four seasons
Making up the One.
The Oneness of the Divine
that shines and shines
through space and time
and beyond space and time.
The infinite … Aleph.

The Four Seasons

Spring, Summer, Autumn, Winter.
Each one a world, a gift.
Each one, divine in wonder.
Physical, spiritual, emotional.
The soul of every season,
is deep and filled with joy.
The buds of Spring,
the Summer bounty,
the Autumn glory, colours changing.
Readiness for wondrous Winter.

The beauty of the gem tones of each season,
How they dance, they move, radiating
with life's romance.

Spring's eagerness to
open fresh to the season's will.
And in sweet Summer.
Summer's colours, bright
and full, and sultry sounds.
The splendour of Autumn.
The scents of leaves transforming,
Winds blow,
as various leaves cascade and twirl.
Snowflakes, Winter. Blue skies, sunshine,
pure white blankets everywhere.
The ice, the wind,
then the stillness of a stunning,
sunny Winter day.
Snow melts. Spring again.

Eetkhuh Metukah
With You Sweetheart

Eetchuh metukah, uhnee tzreekhah
lalekhet li-okyuhnoos
eetkhuh metukah.
boh-oo naylekh yahd bi-yahd
tuhkluht hayarayuhkh mahlah

With you sweetheart.
I need to go to the ocean with you sweetheart.
Let's walk hand in hand under the full moon.

kisheh-haokyanoos meemlahmahl
alainu bikuhltzuhv shellah

As the ocean murmers to us in her rhythm.

eetkhuh metukah
With you sweetheart

uhnee tzreekhah lalekhet li-okyuhnoos!
I need to go to the ocean
with you sweetheart.
Eetchuh metukah.

The Artist's Offering

Spirit painting, cosmic truth.
Universes all unfolding.
What is it that helps give birth to new ideas
inspirations and creations?

May I write a poem, compose a song,
a melody, a picture to help guide you
to your hidden insight?
Here is private invitation
to the depth and loving joy of you.

With gratitude and latitude
artistically, the writer,
the poet, and the educator.
Heaven-sent you are to me indeed.

I'll paint a picture for you.
A picture of your soul.
The universe supplies the download,
and I am just a servant of the divine
who comes to you in humility and gratitude,
humbled by the enormity of
your wondrous presence.
An artist at heart like you
creating life in each moment.

Childhood innocence that ignites
ego-less states, removes judgment and criticism.

I am a Soul Doctor

I am a soul doctor,
I am a physician,
for your spirit, a guide.

Wading from shallow waters
to the deep ocean
of your very essence,
I see your soul,
looking into your
pools of darkness
or pools of light,
shimmering with star sparkle,
back and forth,
like molecules and atoms,
the very elements
in your every
whispered breath.

I am a soul doctor
of your truth,
that hangs from
a tightrope walker's wire,
ensuring it does not dangle,
the frailty of your anchor.

Rest, nourish, exercise
your heartbeat,
soul patient of mine.

I am a soul doctor,
just like you,
a guide to self-healing,
holding your hand,
sitting before you
with compassion and resolve.

To guide you to upgraded
self-healing,
with the queen of medicine,
the king of medicine,
the child of medicine,
love itself, the best
of remedies.

I am a mind and body,
heart and spirit doctor.
Yes, I am a soul doctor,
teacher, medicine messenger of your soul.

Each of us need only embrace
the pure potential
of the maximum possibility
of the moment,
moment by moment.

Healing

Shalom wholeness, peace.
Peace, Love, the Eternal without end.
Ain Sof.
The unspoken name of the divine.
Hashem.
The unspoken name that is felt.
Hashem.
Simkhah! Simkhah. Joy, Joy.
Om Shanti, Om.
Harmony, Peace, Harmony.
Healing. *Marpai.*

Chakras and Sefirot

Hindu teachings, energy centres of creation.
Chakras, wheels of energy.
Life force at play.
Each person adjusts theirs
through insight each day.

Sefirot, Kabbalah teachings, energies of creation.
Spheres or vessels of life's attributes
lived every day.
Each person's life story in Sefirot design
to that which are your gifts
and those that are mine.

Together we share in this world
So divine.

These luminous life pathways
clear truth night and day.
These ancient true teachings
give way to love's crown.
For sacred and Godly practical presence
imbues us with learning
and living life's essence.

Before We Say Goodbye

Before we say goodbye, I want you to know
I'm honoured and I'm humbled.

We share this road together,
in spirit, love and being.
Let's stay connected heart to heart
feeling, sensing, seeing one another one day.
And sharing smiles and stories
through laughter, tears, through song and dance,
with walks in forests by a lake,
the ocean, by a mountain,
along a city street or on a country road,
beneath the bodhi tree or in a synagogue,
a temple or a church.

I'll feel a presence, I will know
your voice, a whisper heard.
If I can help beyond a word I've spoken
just let me know
and I will go inside myself
and reach a little further
for what you need in spirit.

Divine Download for All Souls

From soul spirit to all souls:

"I have loved you long before you came to this Earth,
as you are. You have always been an expression of light,
love, and all possibility to manifest love,
to deepen your connection with your true self,
to witness this within all.
Do not let superficial tendencies erode the true,
beautiful nature of your being.

"Attend to your own birthright of care.
Respect your boundaries and the boundaries of others.
Live freely with compassion,
in health and appreciation,
with creative expression and the genius of you.

"Listen closely to your amazing intuition, igniting your
intelligence, your insight, and your laughter — the
harmony within you. Keep embracing all of you,
all the parts, for you are wholeness, beauty, love,
transformations and stability.

"You are a powerful expression of life and love's
frequencies. Spirit adores you. Spirit loves you.
Dearest one, peace, love, harmony."

Namaste. Shalom.

Peace in the Middle East

We need peace in the Middle East, and in our lives.
Let's take a glimpse into the past—
When Nazis and their collaborators allowed
massacre and destruction,
It was miraculous that Jewish survivors continued to live,
To love, to do life the best they could.

In every country, we taught love, showing respect and courtesy,
Despite the broken lives left behind from the Holocaust.
All nations that have suffered must know: kindness and love
And perseverance towards world peace is the ideal way.
Make this world a place where generations thrive.
Unity and acceptance of diversity, respect for the individual,
And the need for divine and human love to lead.
Action through deep, meaningful conversations with nations,
Finding honest and heartwarming solutions
to difficult situations.

Look to the Middle East for a clear example.
The Jewish people finally returned to their biblical homeland,
As set out by God in the Torah, thousands of years ago.
Palestine, now Israel, since 1948, their ancient home.
Before, hundreds of thousands expelled from Arab countries.
With a history spanning over three thousand years,
They returned to a land of rubble and transformed it.
In 76 years, turned into an oasis built by many,
For all who come to live in this democracy.

Though imperfect, Israel includes Jews,
Christians, and Muslims,
Living freely within its borders.
They uphold what brings true peace—
moral and ethical values.
When neighbours, like those who openly oppress,
May the memories of the departed be a blessing.

May no more war occur,
and may neighbours live in peace.
We must educate ourselves and nations to speak
Of love, healing, and the divine spark within us all.
Living and learning through our commonality.
As eight billion souls, we need universal love,
Building generous, loving relationships with the universe,
With God, with teachings that value all life.
Respect differences, share healthy rituals, and be proud.
Human wonders, imbued with God's blessings.

God awaits our return to goodness, decency, meaningful work.
Shalom aleichem! Salam Salam Alaikem!
To love, to life, to peace!
Connection, heart to heart. Let us laugh together,
Cry together, forgive ignorance, and heal together.
Those who hate have hurts.
Those who love surrender to empathy,
Understanding the missing pieces,
accepting true healing takes time.
Our health, happiness, and hope are in transformation.

Acknowledgments

I WANT TO BEGIN by expressing my gratitude to the Divine Power of the universe, the Source of all life, for granting me the opportunity to share my thoughts and love for all humanity. It is heartbreaking to witness the division in the world, fueled by unexamined media and television reporting, missing facts, and a tendency for many to live unexamined lives. We must educate ourselves with both heart and soul, harnessing our immense capacity to align experience, wisdom, and empathy. It is crucial to recognize how difficult it is to communicate when we allow blind judgment to define our views.

I thank every human being I have met along my journey. Like you, I have felt raw emotions and gained insightful awareness through observation, questioning, and listening to answers both within and without.

I thank the Holocaust survivors and all other survivors of wars from all nations who have shown me what it is to love despite experiencing hatred. I thank all the people who have moved forward from abuse and those who are striving to do so with a willingness to learn. I thank all the children in every country I have visited, whose smiles and delight at life, despite their circumstances, have inspired me to broaden my perspective.

I thank my friends, colleagues, students, professors, teachers, educators, artists, politicians, presidents, authors, human rights and dignity champions, vocational and academic speakers, doctors and nurses, dentists and hygienists, engineers, researchers, scientists, and all sectors of business and human development who have touched my life in significant ways, knowingly and unknowingly, since I was a child.

My family—my mother, sister, grandmother, father, stepfather, aunts, uncles, and cousins—shaped my early experiences of humanitarianism, world peace, love, and equanimity. Our parents survived the Second World War and the Holocaust, teaching us love, care, and discernment. I acknowledge their heroism, often unspoken, that allowed them to move forward.

I thank my neighbours from my childhood community, where we often experienced unity and kindness. Though there were times of disagreement, we mostly succeeded in seeing one another's perspectives through active listening and empathy.

I am grateful for the sacred teachings of the Torah and other ancient and modern teachings from all nations that promote love for all. I thank my teachers at I.L. Peretz School, Jefferson Junior High, Garden City Collegiate, the University of Manitoba, the University of Calgary, Chopra University, the International Pranayama yoga and meditation schools, my Reiki and Intuitive Counseling teachers, my art, music, dance, and theatre teachers, and the clergy from various religions. Their teachings have helped me stay open-minded.

I thank my beloved husband, children, grandchildren, sister, brothers-in-law, sister-in-law, all my in-laws, family, great cousins, and great-great cousins. I also thank my mentors in the community and the world who influence my thoughts on humanitarianism, world peace, universality, and love.

My 94-year-old aunt, who came to Canada as an orphan like my father after World War II, continues to share her wisdom. My grandmother, twice widowed in Europe, exemplified stoic reverence for spirituality, practicality, and deep family love. Her learnedness and love have profoundly influenced me.

I acknowledge the importance of remembering those who came before us and influenced us for good. Everyone has something redeeming, and the best person has flaws. Let us find forgiveness in our hearts for what we do not know and grow in wisdom, learning and doing good for all.

Lastly, I thank my publisher and friend, Dr. Lorene Shyba, for inviting me to expand our award-winning book *Chasia's Enchantment*. Her mastery in various fields and her humility and radiance as a friend are great gifts. I also thank Brianna Haydu and the entire Durvile & UpRoute team of collaborators, authors, speakers, artists, and the marketing and sales team for inspiring the world through stories.

With gratitude and love to you, the readers, may you be inspired to live with hope, faith, curiosity, and the will to examine what is being told in the name of freedom. Freedom belongs to all of us. Absolute freedom is chaos; real freedom is discernment, nourishment, and the embrace of humanity's diversity and unity. Let you be you and me be me, working together to understand with humility, dignity, and love—loads and loads of love in feeling, thought, and action.

— *Hilda Chasia Smith*

DURVILE & UPROUTE BOOKS

DURVILE.COM

"Every River Lit" Series

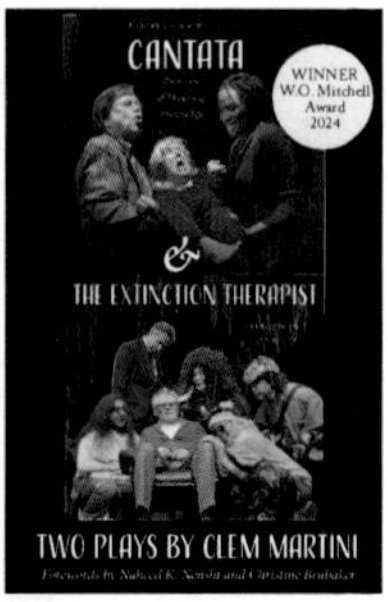

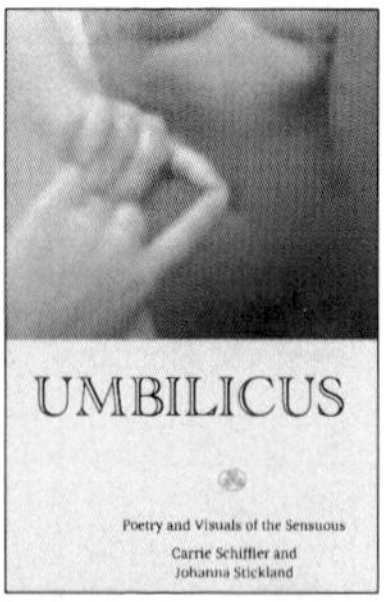

DURVILE & UPROUTE BOOKS
DURVILE.COM

"Ways of Light" Titles

∞

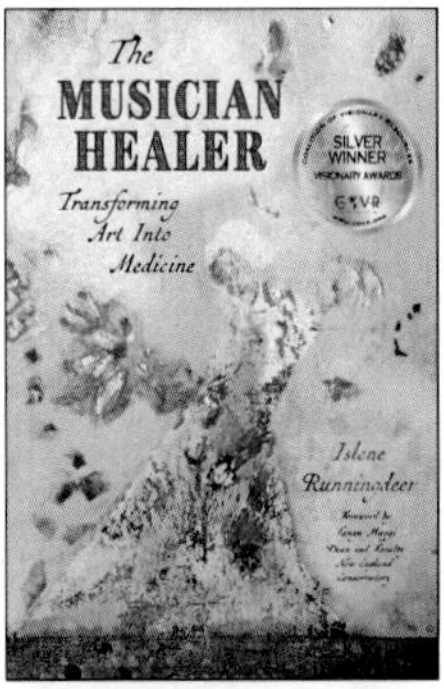

Durvile & UpRoute Books, a small-but-mighty Canadian indie press, publishes print books, e-books, audiobooks, and rich multimedia for enhancement of meaning. Our vision is to inspire authors and artists to bring new knowledge to the world.

Hilda Chasia Smith

Hilda Chasia Szternfeld Smith was born in Winnipeg, Manitoba, Canada, to Holocaust survivors. Her middle name, Chasia, honours her aunt Chasia Goszer, who tragically perished in the Holocaust. Hilda Chasia is a versatile educator, having taught Hebrew, Yiddish, French, and English languages, as well as K-12 education, music, art, meditation, and yoga. She holds degrees from the University of Calgary, the University of Manitoba, Chopra Center University in California, and Pranayama Centers International, founded by Swami Vignanananda. Her prose and poetry have been featured in the *Winnipeg Jewish Post*, the *Calgary Jewish Star*, and in the anthology *Embrace Your Divine Flow: Evolvements for Healing*. Additionally, her music has been incorporated into films and audiobooks, including *The Rainbow, the Midwife & the Birds*. Hilda Chasia's paintings have been showcased in galleries in both Calgary, Alberta and Winnipeg, Manitoba.